Compiled and Arranged By Jim Beloff

HAL•LEONARD®
7777 W. BLUEMOUND RD. P.O. BOX 13819 MILWAUKEE, WI 53213

Edited by Ronny S. Schiff
Cover and Art Direction by Elizabeth Maihock Beloff
Graphics and Music Typography by Charylu Roberts

Foreword

…Welcome to Ukulele Island! Your private island paradise awaits you…where gentle breezes caress the swaying palms. Beneath a cloudless sky, the turquoise waters lap against the sparkling shore and the scent of plumeria perfumes the air. The welcome whirr of the blender beckons with the promise of mai tais back at your shack, but first perhaps a swim, a nap and, of course—a bit of strumming. Ahhh!…

For many, a strummed ukulele can cast quite a spell. Just hearing those soft sounds can conjure up the seductive charms of a tropical island. Once there, you'll want to play some appropriate tunes on your uke, so we've gathered a collection of carefree songs associated with some favorite ports o' call including Hawaii, Jamaica, Brazil and New Zealand. We've also included stops at some imagined locales such as Samba Bay, Margaritaville and even Gilligan's Island.

As with all of our songbooks, we are continually delighted to hear how well different kinds of songs adapt to the ukulele. This time around, the calypso songs of Harry Belafonte, bossa nova of Jobim, reggae of Marley, exotic melody of "The Moon Of Manakoora" and the contemporary pop of Jimmy Buffett and Stephen Bishop all translated beautifully. We've included some strum suggestions here, but these tunes should bring a smile any way you want to play them.

If your current surroundings aren't quite tropical, it is our hope that playing through these songs will be the next best thing to an island vacation. But to get to Ukulele Island you need not wait in long lines at the airport or even rent a car. Just strum those mysterious chords to "Bali Ha'i" and you're in paradise! After all, Ukulele Island is a state of mind.

As always, thank yous to our "audition-ears" who helped us decide on the final song list: Larry Dilg, Mimi Kennedy, Dan Sawyer and Peter Wingerd. Also, special thanks to Liz Beloff, who graphically sets the mood to all of our songbooks and to Charylu Roberts, Ronny Schiff and Hillel Wasserman for all that they do.

—Jumpin' Jim Beloff
Los Angeles, CA 2004

Also Available: (Books) *Jumpin' Jim's Ukulele Favorites; Jumpin' Jim's Ukulele Tips 'n' Tunes; Jumpin' Jim's Ukulele Gems; Jumpin' Jim's Ukulele Christmas; Jumpin' Jim's '60s Uke-In; Jumpin' Jim's Gone Hawaiian; Jumpin' Jim's Camp Ukulele; Jumpin' Jim's Ukulele Masters: Lyle Ritz; Jumpin' Jim's Ukulele Beach Party; Jumpin' Jim's Ukulele Masters: Herb Ohta; Jumpin' Jim's Ukulele Masters: Lyle Ritz Solos; Jumpin' Jim's Ukulele Spirit; Jumpin' Jim's Gone Hollywood; The Ukulele: A Visual History.* **(CDs)** *Jim's Dog Has Fleas; For The Love Of Uke; Lyle Ritz & Herb Ohta—A Night Of Ukulele Jazz.* **(Videos)** *The Joy Of Uke 1; The Joy of Uke 2.*

Visit us on the web at www.fleamarketmusic.com

STRUM SHACK

ISLAND STRUM

Many of the songs in this book can be spiced up with a nice lilting island-y type strum. One that I like to use on "I Can See Clearly Now," "Jamaica Farewell" and "Yellow Bird," is a combination of quick up and down strums plus a roll. In a typical 4-beat measure it would look like this:

⊓ = downstroke
V = upstroke

⊓   *roll* V   ⊓   V   ⊓   V

One and **Two** and **Three** and **Four** and...

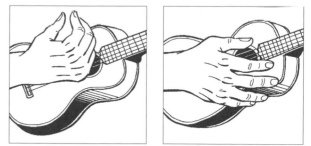

Here's how to make the roll strum.

I play the downstroke with my thumb and the upstroke with my index finger. The roll is made by running the ring, middle and index fingers quickly in succession across the strings.

A variation on this is good for "The Girl From Ipanema," "One Note Samba," "Poinciana" and "Samba Bay."

⊓   *roll* V   V   V

One and **Two** and **Three** and **Four** and...

REGGAE STRUM

Another strum that will come in handy is for reggae-type tunes like Bob Marley's "Three Little Birds." Here, it is all about strumming on the off beat or on the "ands."

⊓ V   ⊓ V   ⊓ V   ⊓ V

One and **Two** and **Three** and **Four** and...

SAMBA STRUM

Use this for a samba like "Brazil." It's a two-meaure pattern.

⊓   ⊓   ⊓   ⊓   ⊓ V   V ⊓

One and **Two** and **Three** and **Four** and **One** and **Two** and **Three** and **Four** and...

CHORD CABANA

Tune Ukulele
G   C   E   A

MAJOR CHORDS

A | A♯/B♭ | B | C | C♯/D♭ | D | D♯/E♭ | E | F | F♯/G♭ | G | G♯/A♭

MINOR CHORDS

Am | A♯m/B♭m | Bm | Cm | C♯m/D♭m | Dm | D♯m/E♭m | Em | Fm | F♯m/G♭m | Gm | G♯m/A♭m

DOMINANT SEVENTH CHORDS

A⁷ | A♯⁷/B♭⁷ | B⁷ | C⁷ | C♯⁷/D♭⁷ | D⁷ | D♯⁷/E♭⁷ | E⁷ | F⁷ | F♯⁷/G♭⁷ | G⁷ | G♯⁷/A♭⁷

DOMINANT NINTH CHORDS

A⁹ | A♯⁹/B♭⁹ | B⁹ | C⁹ | C♯⁹/D♭⁹ | D⁹ | D♯⁹/E♭⁹ | E⁹ | F⁹ | F♯⁹/G♭⁹ | G⁹ | G♯⁹/A♭⁹

MINOR SEVENTH CHORDS

Am⁷ | A♯m⁷/B♭m⁷ | Bm⁷ | Cm⁷ | C♯m⁷/D♭m⁷ | Dm⁷ | D♯m⁷/E♭m⁷ | Em⁷ | Fm⁷ | F♯m⁷/G♭m⁷ | Gm⁷ | G♯m⁷/A♭m⁷

MAJOR SIXTH CHORDS

A⁶ | A♯⁶/B♭⁶ | B⁶ | C⁶ | C♯⁶/D♭⁶ | D⁶ | D♯⁶/E♭⁶ | E⁶ | F⁶ | F♯⁶/G♭⁶ | G⁶ | G♯⁶/A♭⁶

4

MINOR SIXTH CHORDS

Am⁶ → Am^6 | A♯m⁶/B♭m⁶ → $A\sharp m^6 / B\flat m^6$ | Bm⁶ → Bm^6 | Cm⁶ → Cm^6 | C♯m⁶/D♭m⁶ → $C\sharp m^6 / D\flat m^6$ | Dm⁶ → Dm^6 | D♯m⁶/E♭m⁶ → $D\sharp m^6 / E\flat m^6$ | Em⁶ → Em^6 | Fm⁶ → Fm^6 | F♯m⁶/G♭m⁶ → $F\sharp m^6 / G\flat m^6$ | Gm⁶ → Gm^6 | G♯m⁶/A♭m⁶ → $G\sharp m^6 / A\flat m^6$

MAJOR SEVENTH CHORDS

$Amaj^7$ | $A\sharp maj^7 / B\flat maj^7$ | $Bmaj^7$ | $Cmaj^7$ | $C\sharp maj^7 / D\flat maj^7$ | $Dmaj^7$ | $D\sharp maj^7 / E\flat maj^7$ | $Emaj^7$ | $Fmaj^7$ | $F\sharp maj^7 / G\flat maj^7$ | $Gmaj^7$ | $G\sharp maj^7 / A\flat maj^7$

DOMINANT SEVENTH CHORDS WITH RAISED FIFTH (7th+5)

A^{7+5} | $A\sharp^{7+5} / B\flat^{7+5}$ | B^{7+5} | C^{7+5} | $C\sharp^{7+5} / D\flat^{7+5}$ | D^{7+5} | $D\sharp^{7+5} / E\flat^{7+5}$ | E^{7+5} | F^{7+5} | $F\sharp^{7+5} / G\flat^{7+5}$ | G^{7+5} | $G\sharp^{7+5} / A\flat^{7+5}$

DOMINANT SEVENTH CHORDS WITH LOWERED FIFTH (7th-5)

A^{7-5} | $A\sharp^{7-5} / B\flat^{7-5}$ | B^{7-5} | C^{7-5} | $C\sharp^{7-5} / D\flat^{7-5}$ | D^{7-5} | $D\sharp^{7-5} / E\flat^{7-5}$ | E^{7-5} | F^{7-5} | $F\sharp^{7-5} / G\flat^{7-5}$ | G^{7-5} | $G\sharp^{7-5} / A\flat^{7-5}$

AUGMENTED FIFTH CHORDS (aug or +)

Aaug | A♯aug/B♭aug | Baug | Caug | C♯aug/D♭aug | Daug | D♯aug/E♭aug | Eaug | Faug | F♯aug/G♭aug | Gaug | G♯aug/A♭aug

DIMINISHED SEVENTH CHORDS (dim)

Adim | A♯dim/B♭dim | Bdim | Cdim | C♯dim/D♭dim | Ddim | D♯dim/E♭dim | Edim | Fdim | F♯dim/G♭dim | Gdim | G♯dim/A♭dim

Bali Ha'i

Words by
OSCAR HAMMERSTEIN II

Music by
RICHARD RODGERS

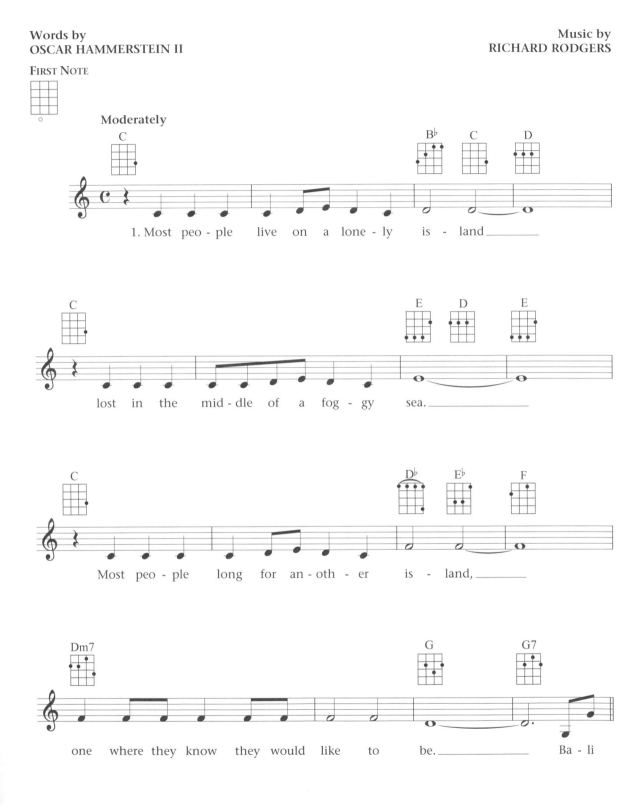

1. Most peo-ple live on a lone-ly is-land lost in the mid-dle of a fog-gy sea.

Most peo-ple long for an-oth-er is-land, one where they know they would like to be. Ba-li

6

Cdim   C   Cdim   C

Ha'i   may   call   you,   an - y   night,   an - y   day.   In   your
2. Ha'i   will   whis - per   on   the   wind   of   the   sea;   "Here   am
3. try,   you'll   find   me   where   the   sky   meets   the   sea,   "Here   am

To Coda ⊕   1.

B   A♭7   C   A♭7   G7   C

heart___   you'll   hear   it   call   you   "Come a - way   Come a - way."   Ba - li
I,___   your   spe - cial   is - land!   Come   to   me,   Come   to
I,___   your   spe - cial   is - land!   Come   to   me,   Come   to

2.
C   F   F+

me!"   Your   own   spe - cial   hopes,   your   own   spe - cial   dreams

Dm   Fm   G7   *D.S. al Coda*

bloom   on   the   hill - side   and   shine   in   the   streams.   If   you

⊕ *Coda*
C   C7   F   G7   C6

me!"   Ba - li   Ha'i   Ba - li   Ha'i   Ba - li   Ha'i. _____

7

The Ballad Of Gilligan's Isle

Words and Music by
SHERWOOD SCHWARTZ and
GEORGE WYLE

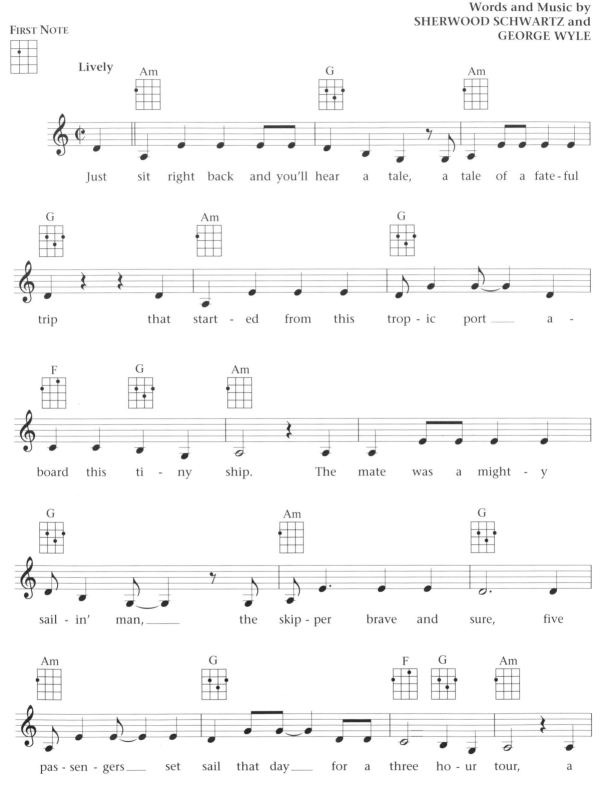

Just sit right back and you'll hear a tale, a tale of a fate-ful trip that start-ed from this trop-ic port ___ a-board this ti-ny ship. The mate was a might-y sail-in' man, ___ the skip-per brave and sure, five pas-sen-gers ___ set sail that day ___ for a three ho-ur tour, a

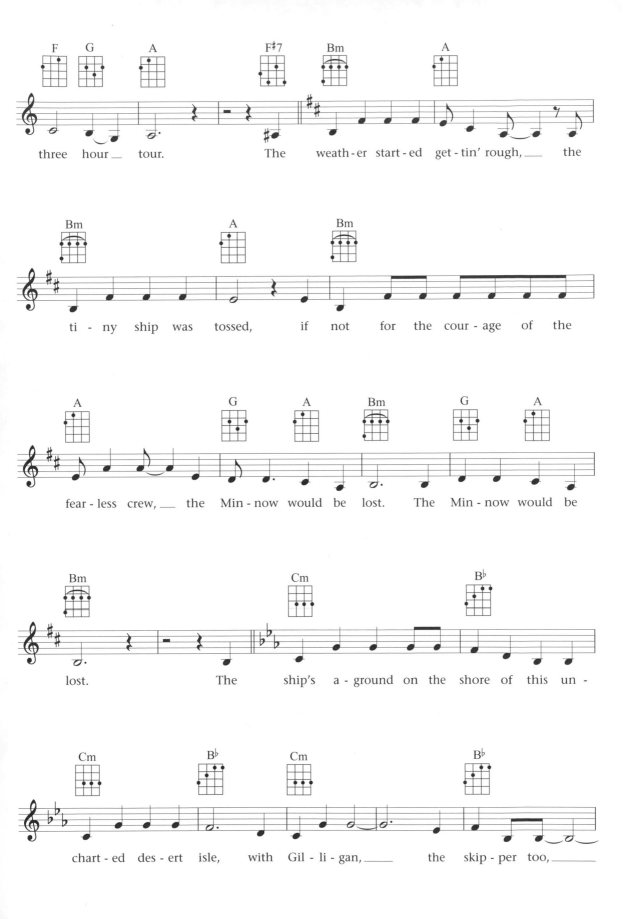

three hour __ tour. The weath-er start-ed get-tin' rough, __ the

ti - ny ship was tossed, if not for the cour-age of the

fear-less crew, __ the Min-now would be lost. The Min-now would be

lost. The ship's a-ground on the shore of this un-

chart-ed des-ert isle, with Gil-li-gan, __ the skip-per too, __

the mil - lion - aire _____ and his wife, _____

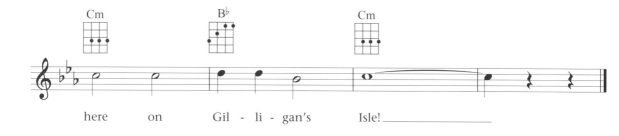

the mov - ie _____ star _____ and the rest _____ are

here on Gil - li - gan's Isle! _____

The cast of the 1960's TV show "Gilligan's Island" (CBS)

Beyond The Sea

**Music and Words by CHARLES TRENET,
ALBERT LASRY and JACK LAWRENCE**

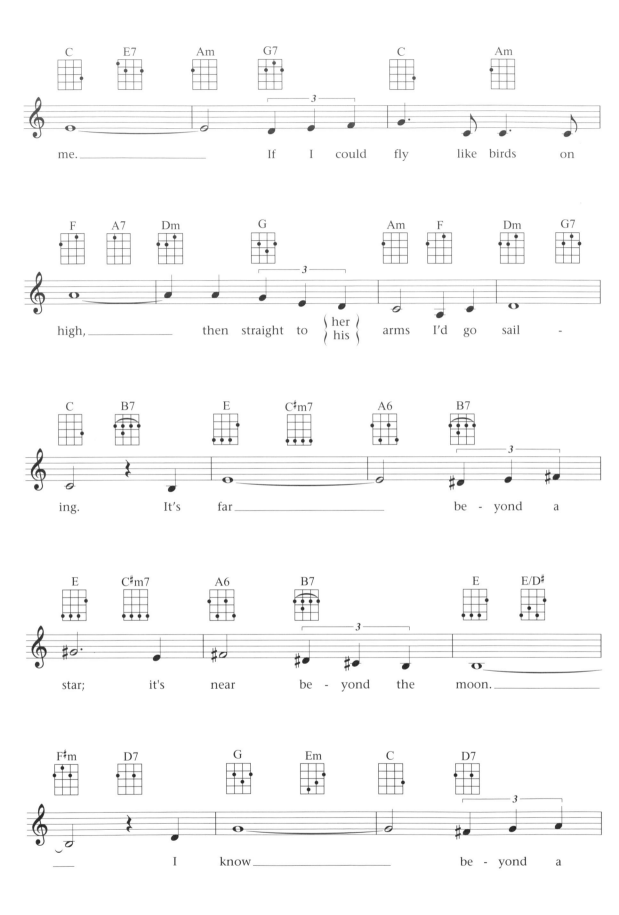

me._____ If I could fly like birds on

high,_____ then straight to { her / his } arms I'd go sail -

ing. It's far_____ be - yond a

star; it's near be - yond the moon._____

___ I know_____ be - yond a

Brazil

English Words by
S. K. RUSSELL

Original Words and Music by
ARY BARROSO

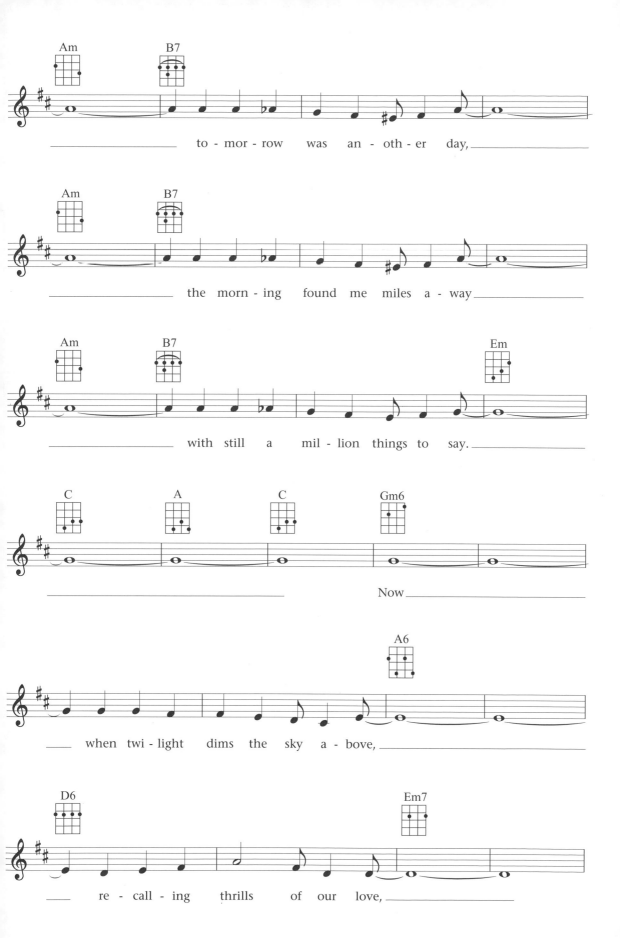

to - mor - row was an - oth - er day,

the morn - ing found me miles a - way

with still a mil - lion things to say.

Now

when twi - light dims the sky a - bove,

re - call - ing thrills of our love,

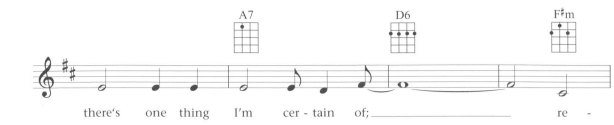

A7   D6   F#m

there's   one   thing   I'm   cer - tain   of;_____   re -

Em7   C#dim   D6   F#m   Em7

turn_____   I   will_____   to   old_____

C#dim   D6

____   Bra - zil._____

Day-O
(The Banana Boat Song)

Words and Music by
IRVING BURGIE and WILLIAM ATTAWAY

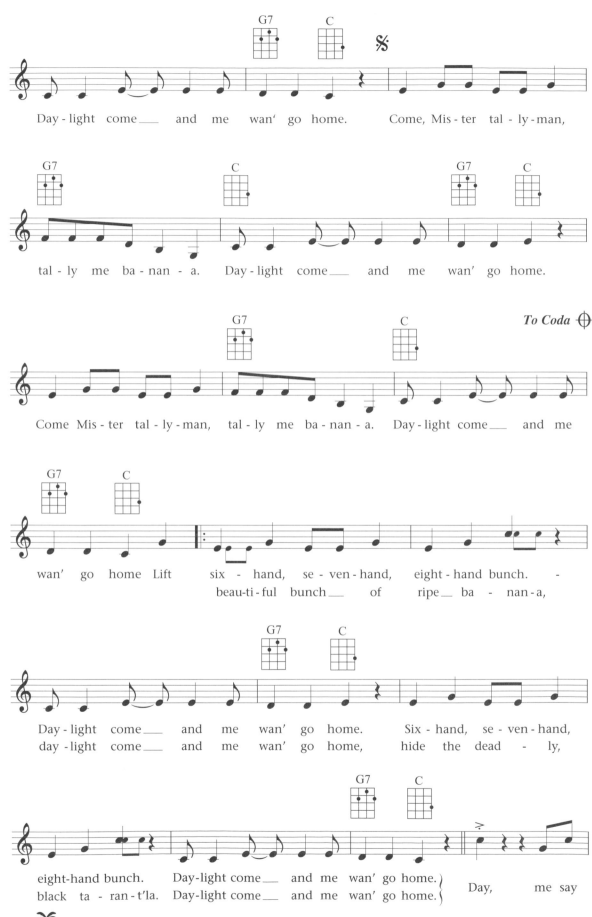

day - o.___ Day-light come___ and me wan' go home. Day, me say,

1. day, me say day, me say day-light come___ and me wan' go home. A

2. *D.S. al Coda* wan' go home.

Coda

wan' go home. Day - o, day - o.___

Day - light come___ and me wan' go home. Day, me say

day, me say day, me say day, me say day, me say day - o.

Day - light come_____ and me wan' go home.

Brown Eyed Girl

Words and Music by
VAN MORRISON

FIRST NOTE

Moderately

Hey, where did we ___ go? Days ___ when the rains ___
___ came, down ___ in the hol - low play - in' a new ___
___ game, laugh - ing and a - run - ning, hey, ___ hey,
skip - ping and a - jump - ing. In the mis - ty morn -
ing fog ___ with our hearts a - thump - in', and

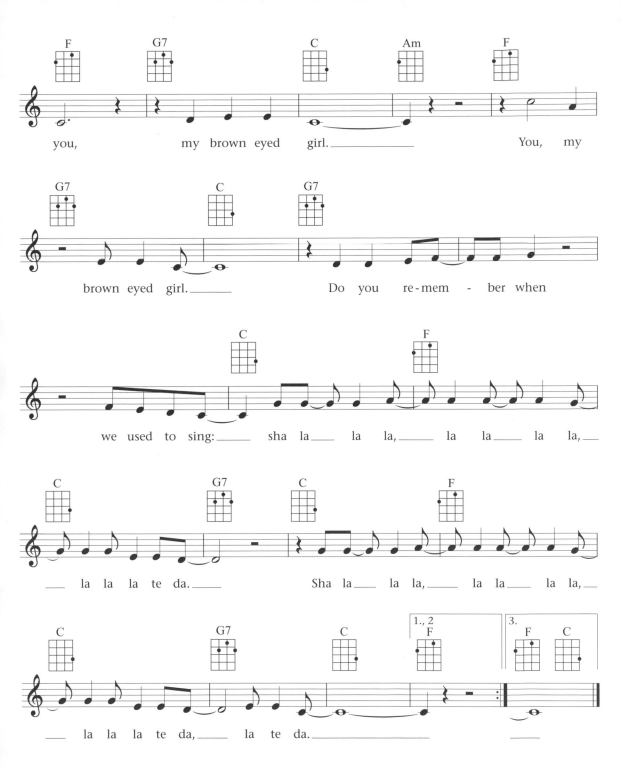

Additional Lyrics

2. Whatever happened to Tuesday and so slow
   going down the old mine with a transistor radio.
   Standing in the sunlight laughing,
   hiding behind a rainbow's wall.
   Slipping and a-sliding,
   all along the waterfall
   with you, my brown eyed girl,
   you, my brown eyed girl.
   Do you remember when we used to sing:
   Chorus

3 So hard to find my way, now that I'm all on my own.
   I saw you just the other day, my, how you have grown.
   Cast my memory back there, Lord;
   sometime I'm overcome thinking 'bout
   making love in the green grass
   behind the stadium,
   with you, my brown eyed girl,
   with you, my brown eyed girl.
   Do you remember when we used to sing:
   Chorus

Don't Worry, Be Happy

Words and Music by
BOBBY McFERRIN

Whistle

Here's a lit - tle song I wrote. ___ You
Ain't got no place to lay ___ your head. ___
Ain't got no cash, ain't got ___ no style. ___

might want to sing it note ___ for note. ___ Don't wor - ry,
Some - bod - y came and took ___ your bed. ___ Don't wor - ry,
Ain't got no gal to make ___ you smile. ___ Don't wor - ry,

be hap - py. In ev - 'ry life we have____
be hap - py. The land - lord say your rent____
be hap - py. 'Cause when you worry your face____

____ some trou - ble, but when you wor - ry you make____
____ is late.____ He may have to lit -
____ will frown____ and that will bring ev'ry - bod -

____ it dou - ble. Don't wor - ry, be hap - py. Don't
i - gate. Don't wor - ry, be hap - py. *Spoken: Look at*____
y down.____ Don't wor - ry, be hap - py. Don't

wor - ry be hap - py now. ⎫
me I'm happy. ⎬ Oo._____ Oo._____
wor - ry be hap - py now ⎭

____ Don't wor - ry, Oo._____ Be hap - py. Oo._____

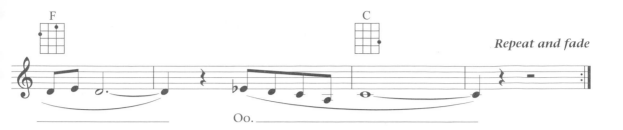

Spoken Ad Lib Over Repeat and Fade

Don't worry. Don't worry. Don't do it.
Be happy. Put a smile on your face.
Don't bring everybody down. Don't worry.
It will soon pass, whatever it is.
Don't worry. Be happy. I'm not worried.
I'm happy.

Enjoy Yourself
(It's Later Than You Think)

Words by
HERB MAGIDSON

Music by
CARL SIGMAN

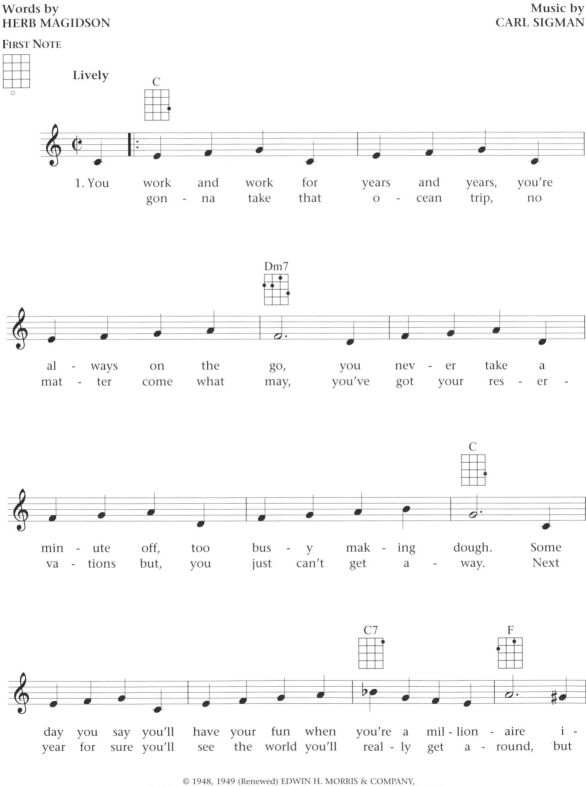

mag - ine all the fun you'll have in your old rock - in' chair. En -
how far can you trav - el when you're six feet un - der - ground.

joy your - self, it's lat - er than you think; en - joy your -

self, while you're still in the pink. The years go

by as quick - ly as a wink, en - joy your - self, en -

joy your - self, it's lat - er than you think. 2. You're lat - er

than you think.

The Girl From Ipanema

English Words by NORMAN GIMBEL
Original Words by VINICIUS DeMORAES

Music by
ANTONIO CARLOS JOBIM

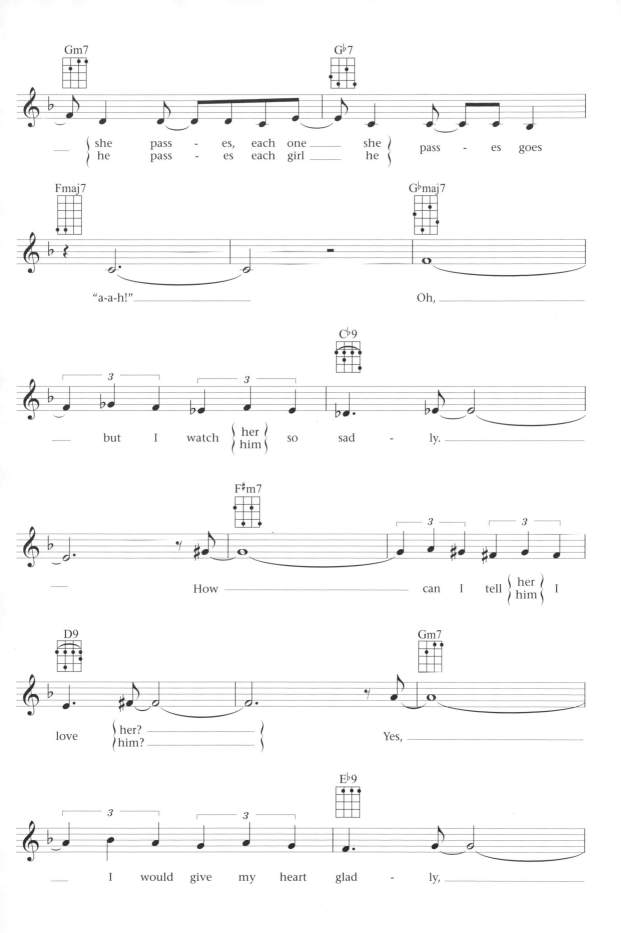

she pass - es, each one _____ she } pass - es goes
he pass - es each girl _____ he }

"a-a-h!" _____ Oh, _____

but I watch { her him } so sad - ly. _____

How _____ can I tell { her him } I

love { her? _____ him? _____ } Yes, _____

___ I would give my heart glad - ly, _____

29

Am7

but   each   day   when { she he } walks   to   the

D7♭9   Gm7

sea,   { she he }   looks   straight   a - head   not   at

C7♭9   Fmaj7

me.   Tall   and   tan   and   young ___

G7

___   and { love - ly, the girl ___ hand - some, the boy ___ }   from   I - pa - ne -

Gm7

ma   goes   walk - ing,   and   when ___   { she he }   pass - es   I   smile,

G♭7   Fmaj7   1. G♭7

___   but { she he } does - n't   see.

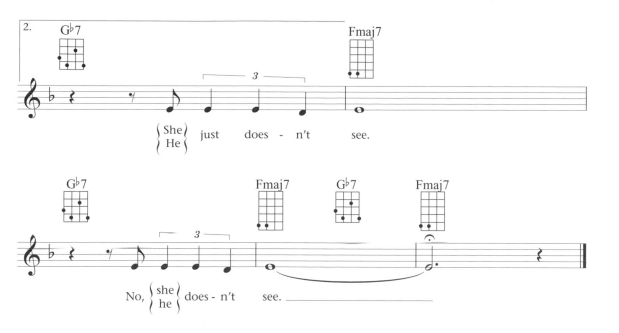

2.

G♭7   Fmaj7

{ She / He } just does - n't see.

G♭7   Fmaj7   G♭7   Fmaj7

No, { she / he } does - n't see.

31

Hanalei Moon

Words and Music by
BOB NELSON

FIRST NOTE

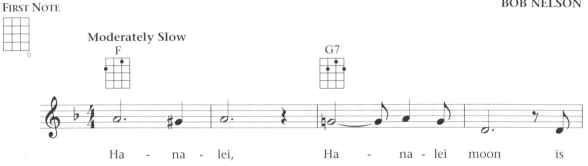

Moderately Slow

Ha - na - lei, Ha - na - lei moon is

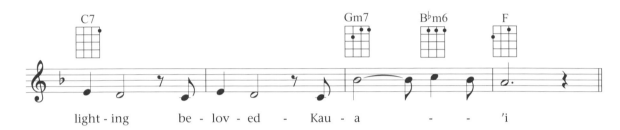

light - ing be - lov - ed - Kau - a - 'i

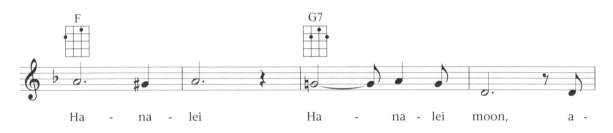

Ha - na - lei Ha - na - lei moon, a -

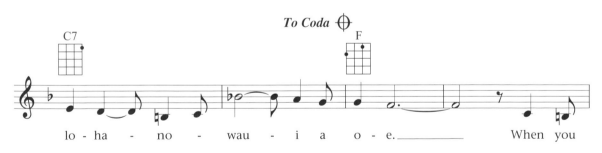

To Coda

lo - ha - no - wau - i a o - e._____ When you

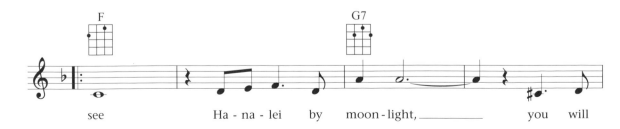

see Ha - na - lei by moon - light,_____ you will

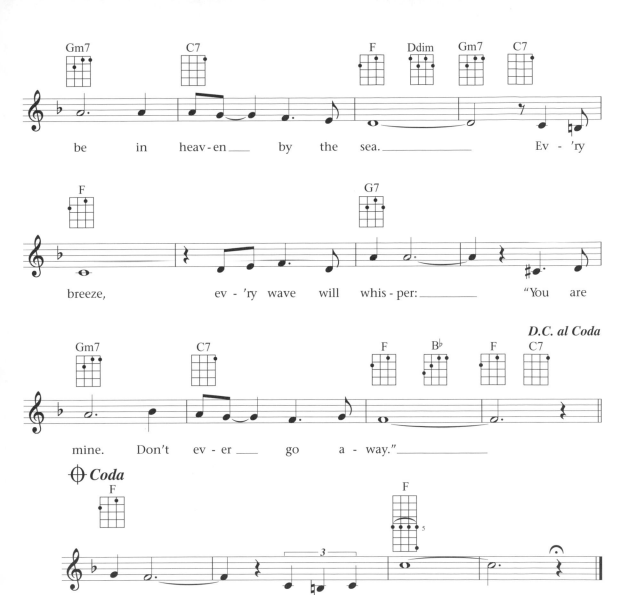

be in heav-en by the sea. Ev - 'ry

breeze, ev - 'ry wave will whis - per: "You are

D.C. al Coda

mine. Don't ev - er go a - way."

Coda

o - e. Ha - na - lei moon.

"POI-O-POI!"

I Can See Clearly Now

Words and Music by
JOHNNY NASH

I'm Carrying A Tiki Torch For You

Words and Music by
Jim Beloff

FIRST NOTE

Con tiki

F   D♭7   C7   F

1. I'm car - ry - ing a ti - ki torch for you,
2. met an - oth - er mai - tai - mak - ing man,
3. car - ry - ing a ti - ki torch for you,

B7   C7   F   D♭7   C7   F

dar - ling, car - ry - ing a ti - ki torch for you.____
dar - ling; does some things with rum that no one can.____
dar - ling. Noth - ing but a ti - ki torch will do.____

F7   B♭   B♭m6   F   E7

—— Sit - ting in this ti - ki bar, won - d'ring dar - ling
—— Now I've got an aw - ful hunch, he has gone and
—— Hop - ing that this flame will be, the light that brings you

To Coda ✛

E♭7   D7   D♭7   C7

where you are, I'm car - ry - ing a ti - ki torch for
spiked your punch, I'm car - ry - ing a ti - ki torch for
home to me.

F   1. D♭7   C7   2. F   F6

you.____
you.____ 2. You   Tro - pic ___ mu -

36

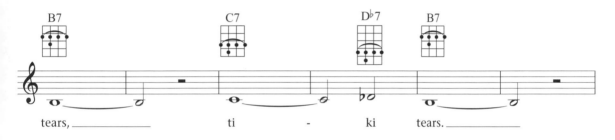
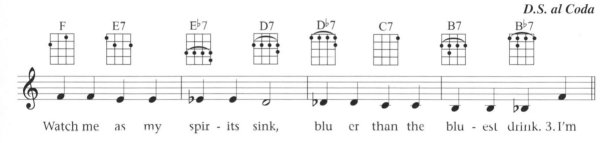
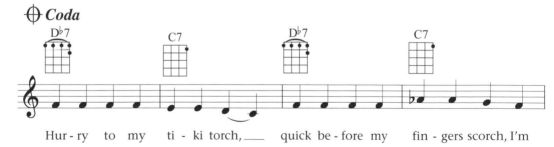
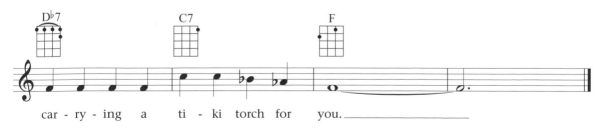

In A Little Hula Heaven

Words and Music by
RALPH RAINGER and LEO ROBIN

FIRST NOTE

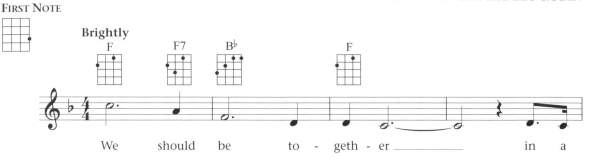

We should be to-geth-er _____ in a

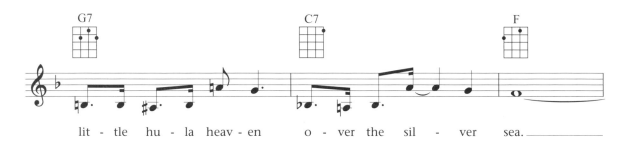

lit-tle hu-la heav-en o-ver the sil-ver sea. _____

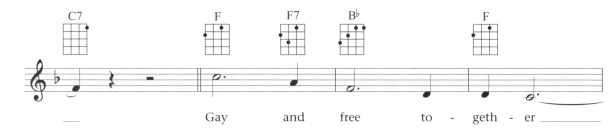

_____ Gay and free to-geth-er _____

_____ in a lit-tle hu-la heav-en un-der a ko-a

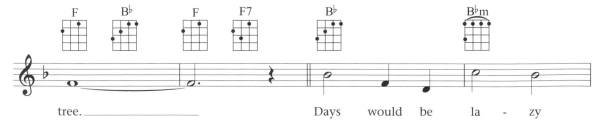

tree. _____ Days would be la-zy

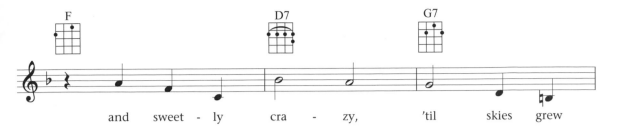

and sweet - ly cra - zy, 'til skies grew

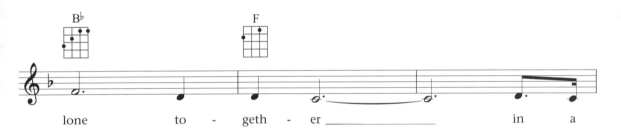

haz - y a - bove. _____ Then we'd be all a -

lone to - geth - er _____ in a

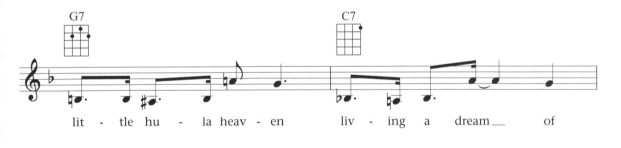

lit - tle hu - la heav - en liv - ing a dream ___ of

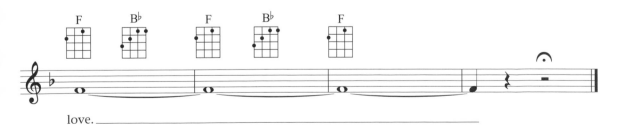

love. _____

Jamaica Farewell

Words and Music by
IRVING BURGIE

1., 4. Down the way where the nights are gay___ and the
2. Sounds of laugh - ter ___ ev - 'ry - where ___ and the
3. Down at the mar - ket ___ you can hear ___ la - dies

sun shines dai - ly on the moun - tain top, ___
danc - ing girls sway - ing to and fro, ___
cry out while on their heads they bear ___

I took a trip on a sail - ing ship ___ and when I
I must de - clare ___ my heart is there, ___ though I've
ac - kie, rice; ___ salt fish are nice, ___ and the

reached Ja - mai - ca, I made a stop. ___
been from Maine ___ to Mex - i - co. ___ } But I'm
rum is fine ___ an - y time of year. ___

sad to say I'm on my way.___ Won't be back for

man - y a day.___ My heart is down,___ my head is

turn-ing a-round,___ I had to leave a lit-tle girl in King - ston town.___

Keep Your Eyes On The Hands

Words and Music by
TONY TODARO and LIKO JOHNSTON

Medium Hula Tempo

When-ev-er you're watch-ing a hu-la girl dance, you got-ta be care-ful you're tempt-ing ro - mance. Don't keep your eyes on her hips, her naugh-ty hu-la hips, just keep your eyes on the hands. Re-mem-ber she's tell-ing a sto-ry to you; her o-pu is sway-ing, but don't watch the view. Don't con-cen-trate on the swing, it does-n't mean a thing,

just keep your eyes on the hands.＿ And when she goes a-round the is-land swing-ing

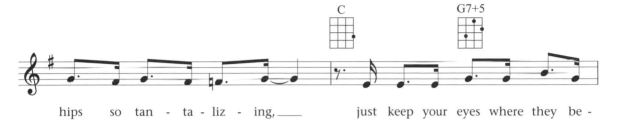

hips   so   tan - ta - liz - ing, ＿＿＿   just keep your eyes where they be -

long,   be-cause the   hu - la has a feel - in' that' - ll   send your sen - ses reel - in', ＿
2. and when her   grass skirt goes a - swish-in', keep your head and don't go wish-in'＿

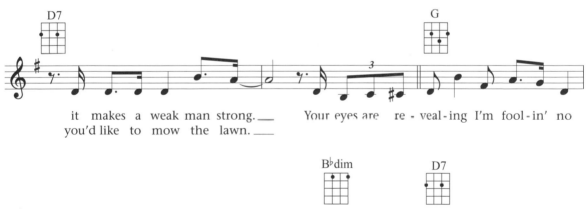

it makes a weak man strong. ＿   Your eyes are re - veal-ing I'm fool-in' no
you'd like to mow the lawn. ＿

one,   no use in con - ceal - ing we're hav - ing some fun.   But if you're

too young to date or o - ver nine-ty-eight,   just keep your eyes on the hands. ＿

43

Limbo Rock

Words and Music by BILLY STRANGE
and JON SHELDON

FIRST NOTE

With a lilt

Ev - 'ry lim - bo boy_____ and girl all a -
First you spread your lim - bo feet, then you

round the lim - bo world; gon - na do the lim - bo rock,
move to lim - bo beat; lim - bo an - kle, lim - bo knee;

all a - round the lim - bo clock.
bend back, like the lim - bo tree. Jack be lim - bo, Jack___ be quick,

Jack go un - der lim - bo stick: all a - round the lim - bo clock,

Fine

hey, let's do the lim - bo rock. *(Spoken:)* "Limbo lower now, limbo lower

now. How low can you go?"   Get your self   a   lim - bo   girl,   give that

chick   a   lim - bo   whirl.   There's   a   lim - bo   moon __ a - bove,

you   will   fall   in   lim - bo   love.   Jack   be

lim - bo,   Jack ___ be   quick,   Jack   go   un - der   lim - bo   stick.

All   a - round   the   lim - bo   clock,   hey, let's   do   the   lim - bo   rock.

D.C. al Fine

(Spoken:) "Don't move that limbo bar. You'll be a limbo star.   How low can you go?"

The Magic Islands

Traditional Polynesian Melody
"Ku'u Lei Awapuhi"
Lyrics and Adaptation by
KEN DARBY

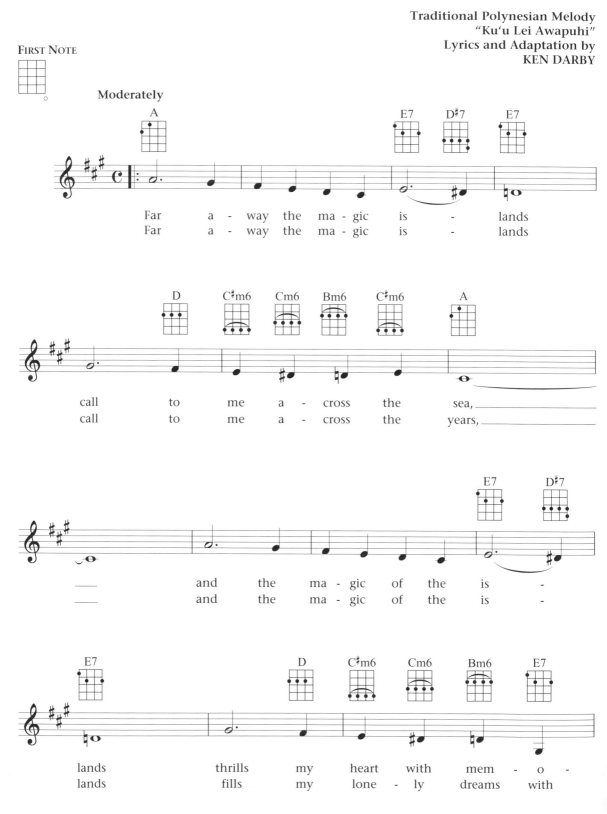

Far a - way the ma - gic is - lands
Far a - way the ma - gic is - lands

call to me a - cross the sea,
call to me a - cross the years,

and the ma - gic of the is -
and the ma - gic of the is -

lands thrills my heart with mem - o -
lands fills my lone - ly dreams with

ry. _____

tears. _____ White gin - ger was in bloom, _____

___ it filled the air _____ with sweet per -

fume and we were there. _____

___ Two sha - dows on the sand, _____ a tro - pic moon a -

bove _____ and we were lost, so lost in

1.
love. _____

2.
love. _____

Margaritaville

Words and Music by
JIMMY BUFFETT

*Uke players might want to substitute "four" string.

Wast - in' a - way a - gain___ in Mar - ga - ri - ta - ville,

search - in' for my___ lost sha - ker of salt.___

___ Some__ peo -ple claim___ that there's__ a

wom - an to blame,_____ { but I know___ now I think___ but I know___

Fine   *D.C. al Fine*

{ it's no - bod - y's fault.____ hell, it could__ be my fault.____ it's my own__ damn__ fault.____ }

Marianne
(All Day, All Night, Marianne)

Words and Music by TERRY GILKYSON,
RICHARD DEHR and FRANK MILLER

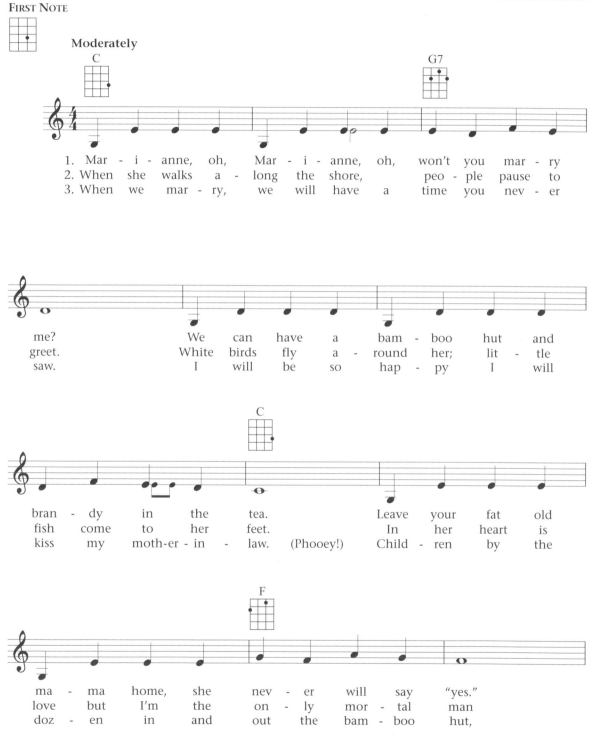

1. Mar - i - anne, oh, Mar - i - anne, oh, won't you mar - ry
2. When she walks a - long the shore, peo - ple pause to
3. When we mar - ry, we will have a time you nev - er

me? We can have a bam - boo hut and
greet. White birds fly a - round her; lit - tle
saw. I will be so hap - py I will

bran - dy in the tea. Leave your fat old
fish come to her feet. In her heart is
kiss my moth - er - in - law. (Phooey!) Chil - dren by the

ma - ma home, she nev - er will say "yes."
love but I'm the on - ly mor - tal man
doz - en in and out the bam - boo hut,

If ma - ma don't know now, she can guess. My, my, yes.
who's al - lowed to kiss my Mar - i - anne. Don't rush me.
one for ev - 'ry palm tree and cok - y - nut. Hur-ry up now.

All day, all night, Mar - i - anne,_____

down by the sea - side sift - in' sand._____

E - ven lit - tle chil - dren love Mar - i - anne,_____

1., 2.

_____ down by the sea - side sift - in' sand._____

3.

sift - in' sand._____

The Moon Of Manakoora

Words by
FRANK LOESSER

Music by
ALFRED NEWMAN

The moon of Man - a - koo - ra filled___ the night, with
ma - gic Pol - y - ne - sian charms,___ the
moon of Man - a - koo - ra came___ in sight, and
brought you to my ea - ger arms.___ The
moon of Man - a - koo - ra soon___ will rise, a -

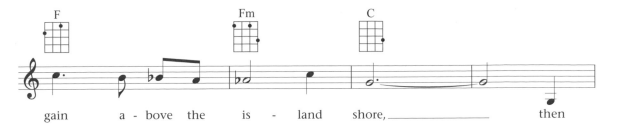

F   Fm   C

gain   a - bove   the   is - land   shore, _____ then

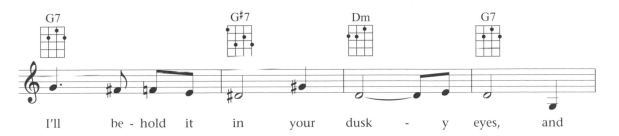

G7   G#7   Dm   G7

I'll   be - hold   it   in   your   dusk - y   eyes,   and

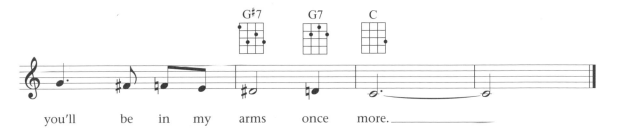

G#7   G7   C

you'll   be   in   my   arms   once   more. _____

Now Is The Hour
(Maori Farewell Song)

Words and Music by MAEWA KAITHAU,
CLEMENT SCOTT, and DOROTHY STEWART

FIRST NOTE

Slowly

Sun - set glow fades in the west; _____

night o'er the val - ley is creep - ing.

Birds cud - dle down in their nest; _____

soon all the world will be sleep - ing. And now

is the hour _____ when we must say good -

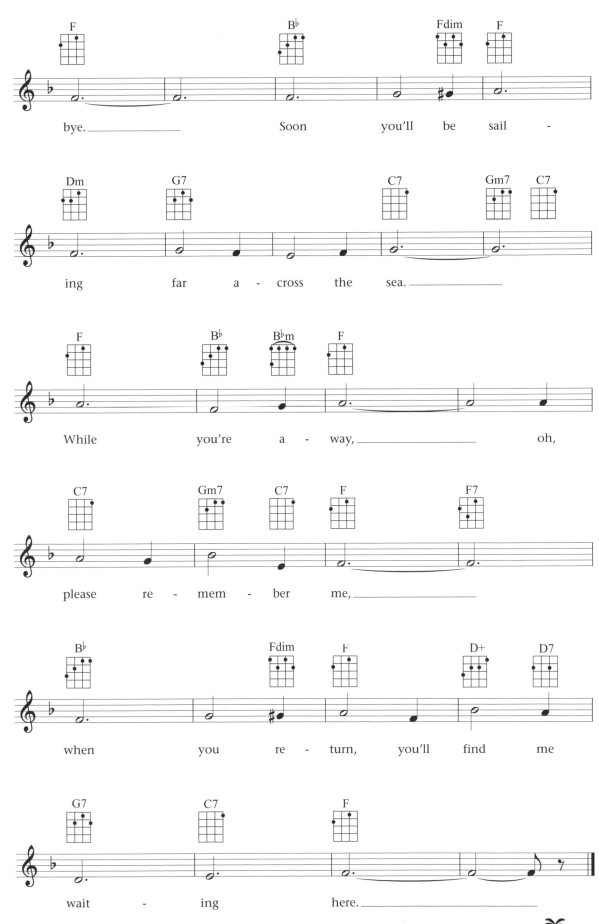

bye._____ Soon you'll be sail -

ing far a - cross the sea._____

While you're a - way, _____ oh,

please re - mem - ber me, _____

when you re - turn, you'll find me

wait - ing here._____

FLORIDA

CUBA

NASSAU

BAHAMA ISLANDS

JAMAICA

HAITI

DOMINICAN REP.

Caribbean Sea

DON THE BEACHCOMBER

XXX RUM

PUERTO RICO

VIRGIN ISLANDS

GUADELOUPE

MARTINIQUE

BARBADOS

On And On

Words and Music by
STEPHEN BISHOP

FIRST NOTE

Moderately

Down in Ja - mai - ca they got lots of pret - ty wom - en.
Poor ol' Jim - my sits a - lone in the moon - light.___
sun on my shoul - ders and my toes in the sand.

Steal your mon - ey, then they break your heart.___
Saw his wom - an kiss an - oth - er man. __ So he
Wom - an's left me for some oth - er man.___ Ah, but

Lone - some Sue, she's in love with ol'___ Sam. __ Take___
takes a lad - der; steals the stars from the___ sky.___
I don't care. I'll just dream and stay___ tan.___

___ him from the fire in - to the fry - ing pan.___ On and
Puts on Si - na - tra and___ starts to cry.___ On and
Toss up my heart___ to see where it lands.___ On and

Dm7   G7sus   G7

on,   she   just   keeps_____   on   try - ing._____
on,   he   just   keeps_____   on   try - ing._____
on,   I   just   keep_____   on   try - ing._____

Cmaj7   A7sus   A7

And   she   smiles_____   when   she   feels_____   like   cry - ing.   On_____
And   he   smiles_____   when   he   feels_____   like   cry - ing.   On_____
And   I   smile_____   when   I   feel_____   like   dy - ing.   On_____

To Coda ⊕

Dm7   G7sus   G7   C   Am

_____ and on,   on   and   on,   on_____   and   on._____
_____ and on,   on   and   on,   on_____   and   on._____
_____ and on,   on   and   on,   on_____   and   on._____

1.   C   Am   2.   C   Am   Fmaj7

When   the   first   time_____   is   the   last___

Em7   Dm7   G7sus   Cmaj7

_____ time,_____   it   can   make   you   feel_____   so   bad._____   But   if   you

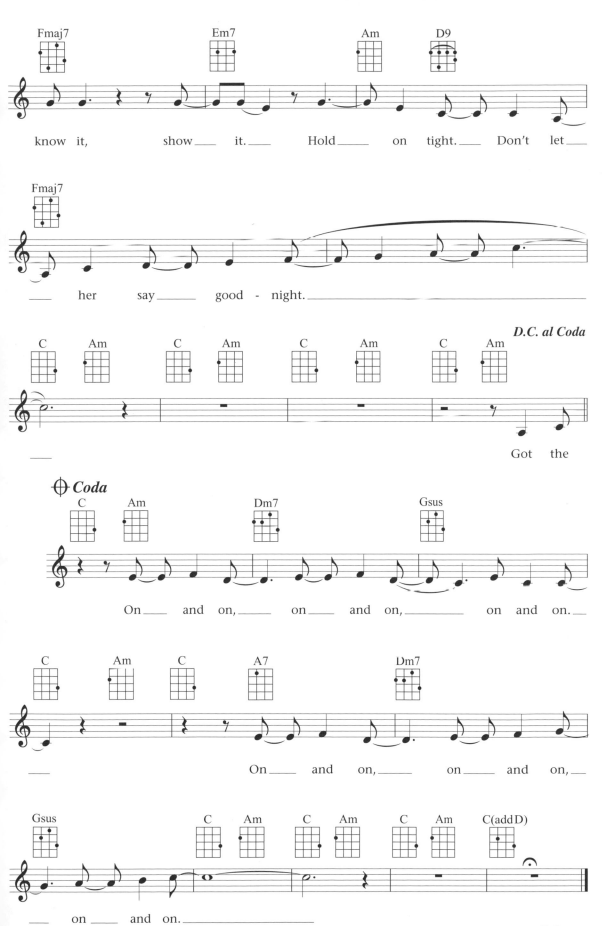

know it, show it. Hold on tight. Don't let

her say good - night.

D.C. al Coda

Got the

Coda

On and on, on and on, on and on.

On and on, on and on,

on and on.

On A Slow Boat To China

Words and Music by
FRANK LOESSER

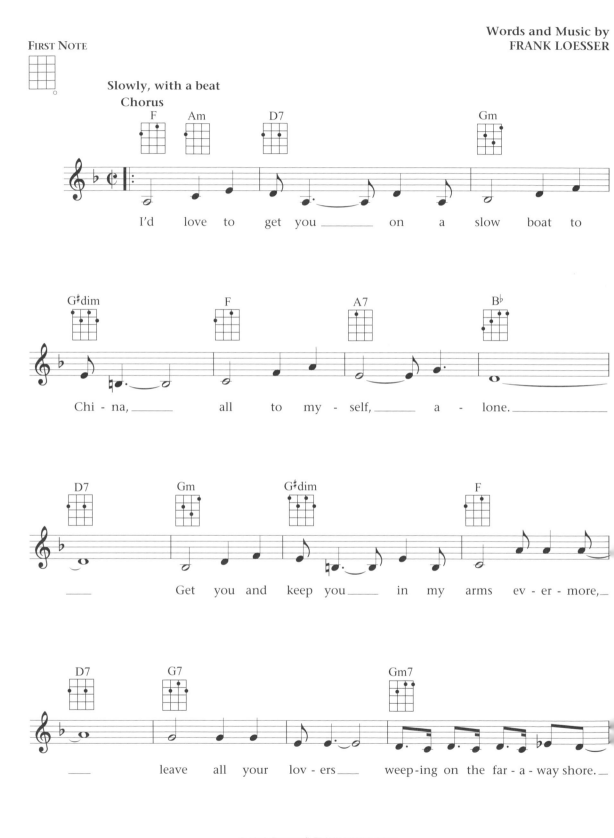

60

Out on the bri - ny   with   a   moon   big   and

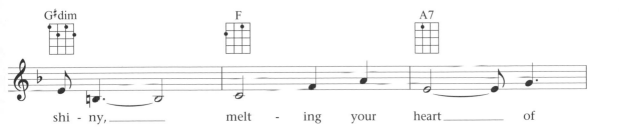

shi - ny,   melt - ing   your   heart   of

stone,   I'd   love   to   get you,   on   a

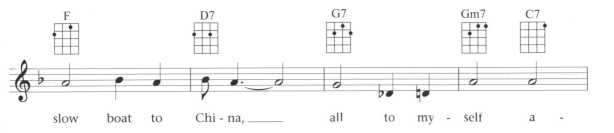

slow   boat   to   Chi - na,   all   to   my - self   a -

Fine

lone.   There   is   no   verse   to   this   song

D.C. al Fine

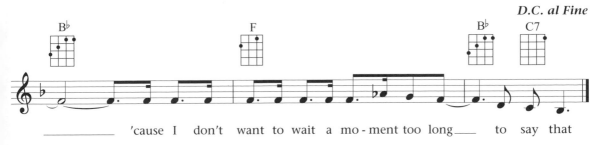

        'cause   I   don't   want   to   wait   a   mo - ment   too   long   to   say   that

One Note Samba
(Samba Du Uma Nota So)

Original Words by
NEWTON MENDONCA

English Words and Music by
ANTONIO CARLOS JOBIM

FIRST NOTE

Lightly, with movement

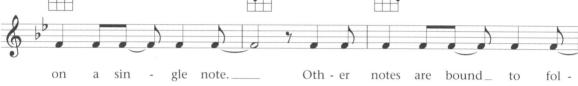

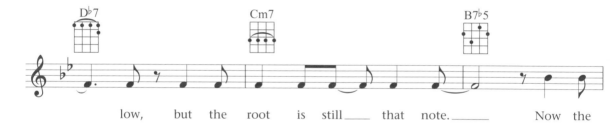

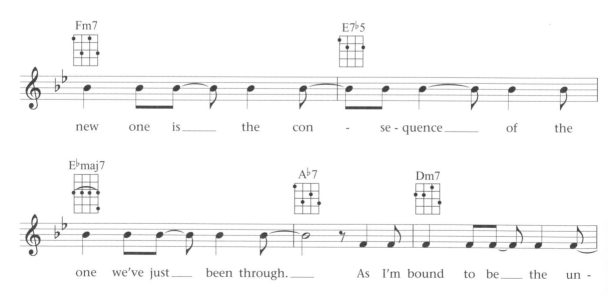

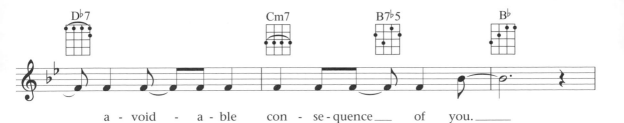

a - void - a - ble con - se - quence____ of you._____

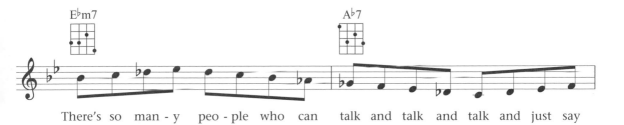

There's so man - y peo - ple who can talk and talk and talk and just say

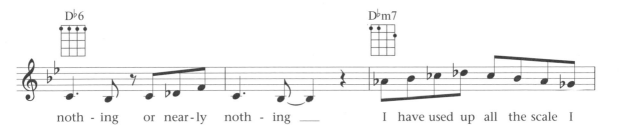

noth - ing or near - ly noth - ing ____ I have used up all the scale I

know and at the end I've come to noth - ing, or near - ly

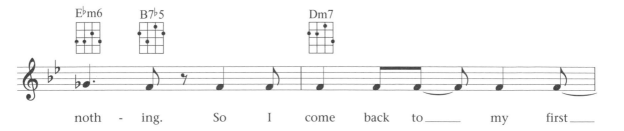

noth - ing. So I come back to_____ my first____

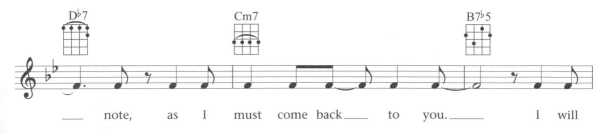

____ note, as I must come back____ to you._____ I will

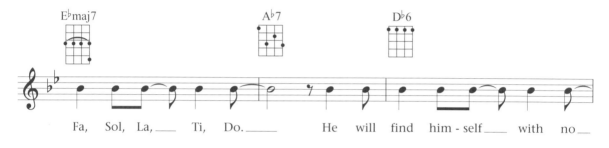

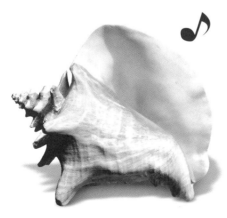

Poinciana
(Song Of The Tree)

Words by
BUDDY BERNIER

Music by
NAT SIMON

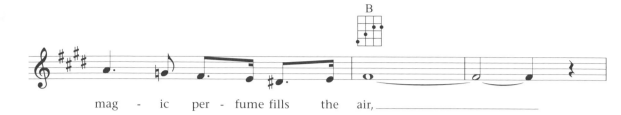

mag - ic per - fume fills the air,

to and fro you sway, my heart's in time, I've learned to care.

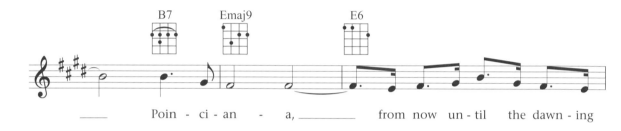

____ Poin - ci - an - a, ____ from now un - til the dawn - ing

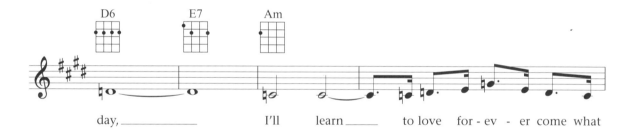

day, ____ I'll learn ____ to love for - ev - er come what

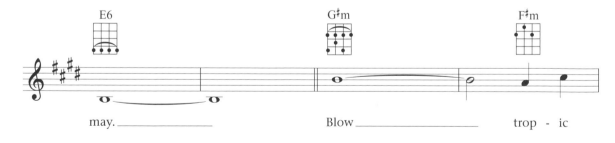

may. ____ Blow ____ trop - ic

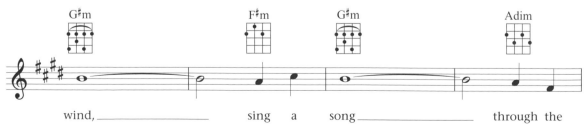

wind, ____ sing a song ____ through the

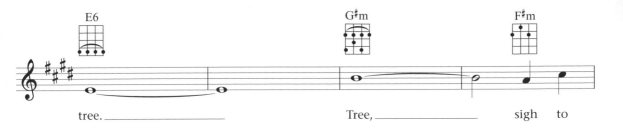

E6   G#m   F#m

tree. _____ Tree, _____ sigh to

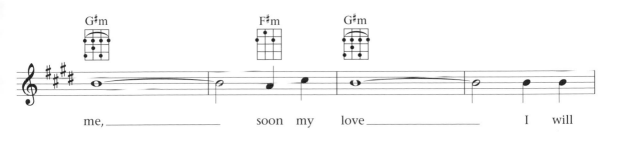

G#m   F#m   G#m

me, _____ soon my love _____ I will

E6

see. _____

Samba Bay

Words by
JIM BELOFF

Music by
HERB OHTA

FIRST NOTE

1. In the mid - dle of _____ a great _____ big o - cean lies _____ an is - land full _____ of mo - tion, where _____ the peo - ple dance _____ the day _____ a - way. _____ Should _____ you ev -

2. find that their _____ com - mun - i - ca - tion, is _____ a kind _____ of syn - co - pa - tion, peo - ple talk _____ with ev - 'ry swing _____ and sway. _____ Should _____ you have _____

er ship - wreck on_____ this is - le, be
some things _____ in need_____ of say - ing, bet -

_____ pre - pared_____ to stay _____ a - whi - le; you _____
ter get _____ your hips _____ a - sway - ing, they_____

1.
_____ have stum - bled on - to Sam - ba Bay. _____

2.
Here you'll _____ speak sam - ba down _____

_____ in Sam - ba Bay. _____

Sway
(Quien Sera)

English Words by
NORMAN GIMBEL

Spanish Words and Music by
Pablo Beltran Ruiz

When ma - rim - ba rhy-thms start to play, dance with me, make me sway.___ Like the la - zy o - cean hugs the shore, hold me close, sway me more._____ Like a flow - er bend-ing in the breeze, bend with me, sway with ease.___ When we dance you have a way with me, stay with me,

Three Little Birds

Words and Music by
BOB MARLEY

ris - ing sun. Three___ lit - tle birds___ pitch by my

door - step, sing-in' sweet___ songs of mel - o - dies

pure and true, say - in', "This is my mes - sage to you -

1. u - u." Sing - in', "Don't 2. u - u." Sing - in', "Don't

wor - ry a - bout a thing.___ 'cause

Repeat and Fade

ev - 'ry lit - tle thing gon - na be al - right."___ Sing - in', "Don't

73

Volcano

Words and Music by
JIMMY BUFFETT, KEITH SYKES
and HARRY DAILEY

FIRST NOTE

Moderate Reggae

I don't___ know,   I don't___ know

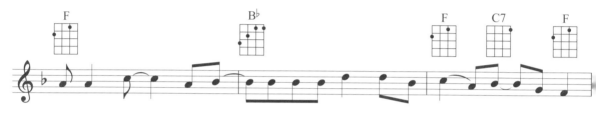

I don't know___ where I'm   a-gon-na go when the vol - ca - no blow.

1.
2.
Let me say it now:

1. Ground, she's mov-in'   un - der me.
2. my girl quick-ly   said to me,
3. No time to count___   what I'm worth,

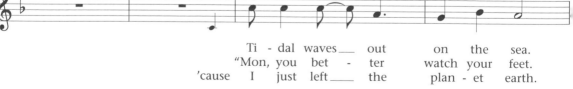

Ti - dal waves___ out   on the sea.
"Mon, you bet - ter   watch your feet.
'cause I just left___ the   plan - et earth.

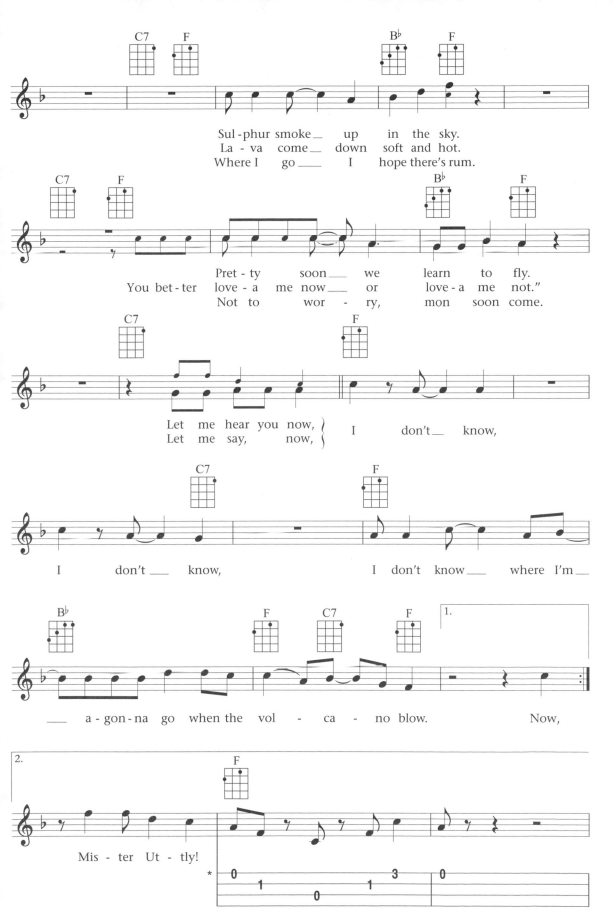

Sul-phur smoke___ up in the sky.
La-va come___ down soft and hot.
Where I go___ I hope there's rum.

Pret-ty soon___ we learn to fly.
You bet-ter love-a me now___ or love-a me not."
Not to wor-ry, mon soon come.

Let me hear you now, ⎰
Let me say, now, ⎱ I don't___ know,

I don't___ know, I don't know___ where I'm___

___ a-gon-na go when the vol-ca-no blow. Now,

Mis-ter Ut-tly!

*Ukulele tablature: the 4 lines here correspond to the four uke strings with the A string on top.
The numbers represent the frets (O means open string). Play in the same rhythm shown in staff above.

One more now, I don't __ know,

I don't __ know, I don't know __ where I'm __

__ a - gon - na go when the vol - ca - no blow. But I

4. don't want to land __ in New York Cit - y, I don't want to land __ in
5. don't want to land __ in Com - man - che Sky Park, __ or in Nash - ville,
6. don't want to land __ no San - Di - e - go, __ don't want to land __ no

Yellow Bird

Words by
ALAN and MARILYN BERGMAN

Music by
NORMAN LUBOFF

1. Yel - low bird, up high in ba - na - na tree. Yel - low bird, you sit all a - lone like me. Did your la - dy frien' leave de nest a - gain? Dat is ver - y sad, make me feel so bad. You can fly a - way, in the sky a - way. You more luck - y dan me!

2. Yel - low bird, up high in ba - na - na tree. Yel - low bird, you sit all a - lone like me. Bet - ter fly a - way in de sky a - way. Pick - er com - in' soon, pick from night to noon. Black an' yel - low you, like ba - na too. Dey might pick you some day!

Dm7   G7

I al - so ___ have a pret - ty gal, ___ she not with ___ me to -
Wish dat I ___ was a yel - low bird, ___ I fly a - way with

C   Dm7

day.   Dey all de ___ same, de pret - ty gal, ___
you.   But I am ___ not a yel - low bird, ___

G7   Dm7   G7   C

make dem ___ de nest, den dey fly a - way. ___
so here ___ I sit, noth - in' else to do! ___

Song Of The Islands

Words and Music by
CHAS. E. KING

FIRST NOTE

Moderately, in a flowing style

C   C#dim   G7   D7   G7

Ha - wai - ian isles of beau - ty, ____ where skies are blue and love is

C   A7   D7

true; ____ where balm - y airs and gold - en moon - light ____ ca - ress the

G7   C   C#dim

wav - ing palms of Ho - no - lu - lu. Your val - leys with their

G7   D7   G7   C

rain - bows ____ your moun - tains green, the a - zure sea. ____ Your fra - grant

A7   D7   G7   C

flow'rs, en - chant - ing mu - sic ____ u - nite and sing a - lo - ha oe to me.